Contents

MEET THE AUTHOR

SIMONE LIA

Creator of SAUSAGE AND CARROTS

LOVES: butterflies, hermits and riding my bike.

HATES: being squashed, loud noises and sticky tables.

BY

ROBIN ETHERINGTON & ZAK SIMMONDS-HURN

Yeah, Ruby. This'll be fun!
Hmm.
SKID

Hello children. Step inside and see yourselves as never before.
Horrible kids! Always touching my lovely clean mirrors with their sticky fingers. Well not this time! Ha ha!

I take it back. He is creepy.
I told you so!
Oh come on, you two.
It's supposed to be fun!
FLIP

Inside the Hall of Mirrors.

I'm not so sure about this.

What a weird place.

I like it! The mirrors make you look a funny shape, and they move!

OK then, funniest body shape wins a large bucket of popcorn.

DON'T TOUCH

HANDS OFF!

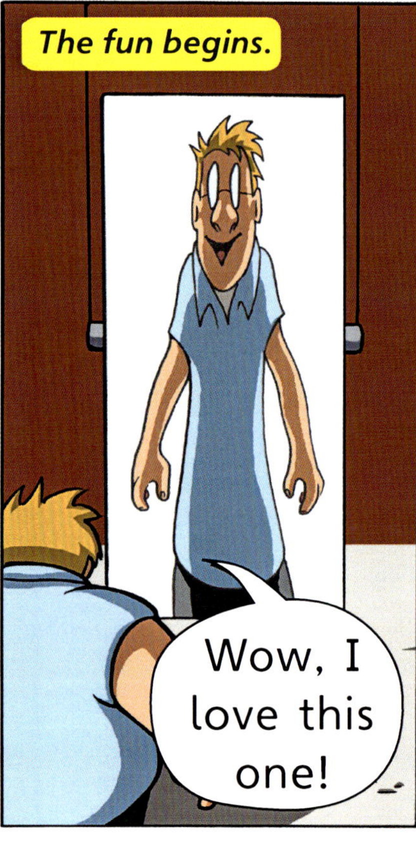

What have the children seen? Find out on page 12.

CRAB LANE CREW
BY JIM MEDWAY
Hey! What are you doing?
What's that stuff for?
PLASTER

Follow us and you'll see.
What's this book?

"Tracking and Trailing".
Hey!
What is it?

Just help us look for animal tracks.
OK.
What are tracks?
PLASTER

Tracks are footprints, Mark.
Are we going to follow them home? And ask for lunch?

Stop being silly, Mark!
He's only joking!
PLASTER
Hey look!
Tracks?
Over there!

Wow, cool! I bet it's a fox.
Let's look in the book.

So what's this stuff for, then?
Watch and learn!

We mix up some plaster, then make little card rings, like this.

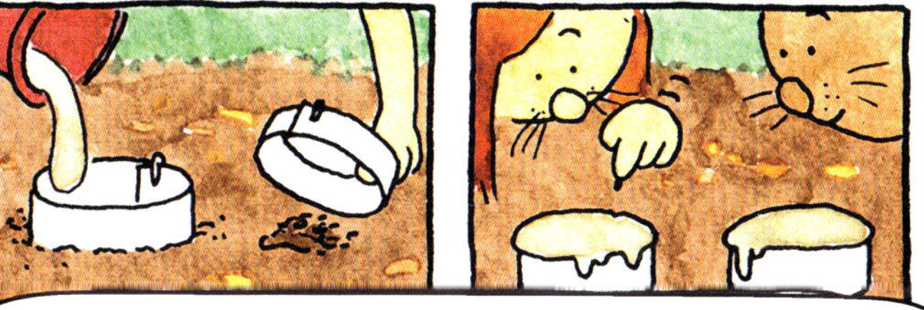
Then you pour it in and leave it to set for a minute or two.

Wow! Can I hold it?
Don't drop it.
Stop being bossy!

It looks exactly like a pawprint.
That's really clever.

Hey look! You can make your own animal prints with this!
Wow!

I bet we could trick Chris and Ahmed.
Hey, I've got a plan!

Later that day…
Hey Chris! Ahmed!
We've found more animal tracks!

Good work, Claire!
Hey, they look fresh!
Let's follow them.

Wow! How did it do that?
Wait, look!

Tyre tracks!

What's that?

GASP!

Help, help! Someone call a vet, quick!

I think I've broken my paw! Hee hee hee!

Could you put it in plaster for me?
Ha ha!
Hee hee!
We've been tricked.
Hmph.

TRACKING ANIMALS

Tracking means following animals by the marks they leave.

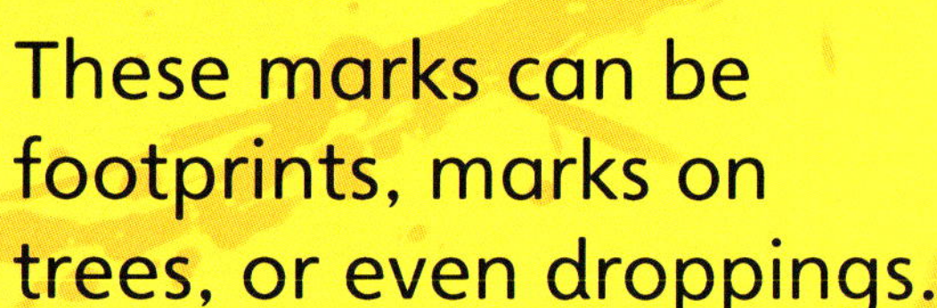

These marks can be footprints, marks on trees, or even droppings.

The marks show you which animals have been in the area. They also show you where they might have gone.

If you want to be a good tracker you need to learn what animal footprints look like. You can get a book from the library to help you.

Make sure you look out for droppings, too. Each animal leaves different droppings.

Animals leave clues on plants and trees, too. Some animals flatten plants or rub up against trees and leave marks. Others eat tree bark.

Can you match up the animal to the tracks it leaves? Try this test.

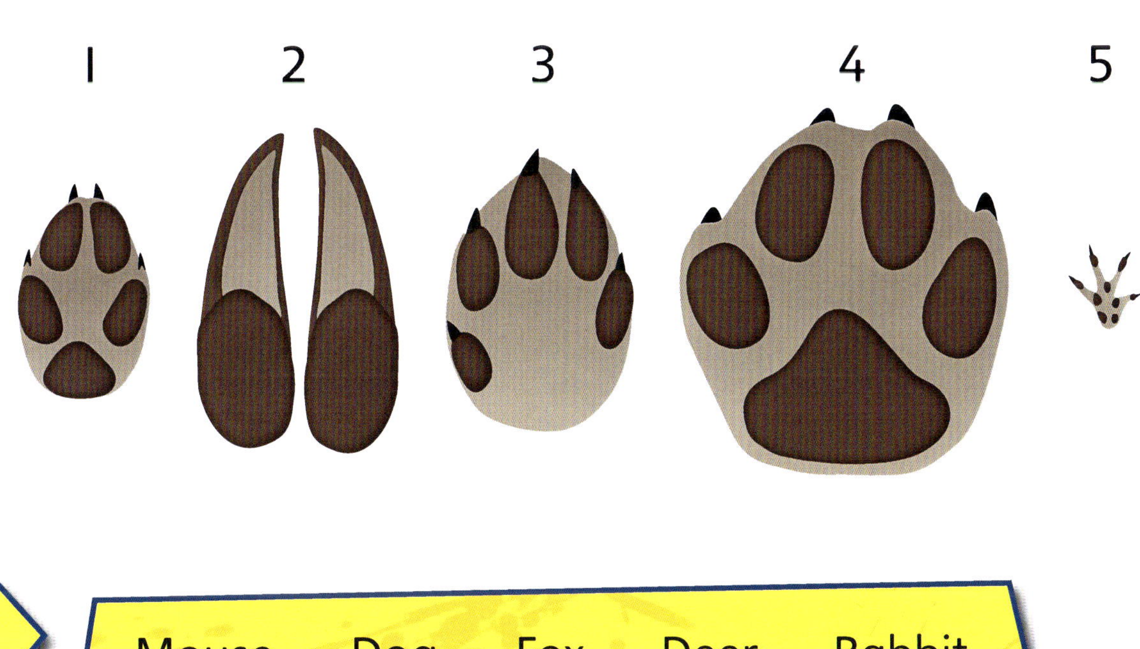

Mouse Dog Fox Deer Rabbit

Answers: 1. fox 2. deer 3. rabbit 4. dog 5. mouse

BY

ROBIN ETHERINGTON & ZAK SIMMONDS-HURN

Friends Franky, Ruby and Edi have discovered something strange in the Hall of Mirrors …

If we're going to save Franky and the others we need to clear a path. These moving mirrors are putting me off.

Get your head down, Edi.
Yikes!
Watch this!

KRAK
SHATTER
SMASH
Woah! Good shot!
Thanks!

Smashing this mirror might hurt the kids.
But how can we get them out?
SCREEEEEECH
GRAB

Of course!

Think fast, Ruby! I'm starting to feel hungry and all I can think about is a hot dog with lots of tomato sauce.

What?
That's it! When there's a little bit of tomato sauce left in the bottle and it won't come out, what do you do?
You give it a good whack!
SWING

And so ...
Harder Edi!
I hope this works!
JUMP
THUMP

CREEEEEEEAK
I think it's working!

SHUUUUUUUUUP
Yeah!
Woah!

Just then …
My mirrors! I told you kids to not touch them!

But how did you escape? What are you doing?

It's time you had a taste of your own medicine!
No, please!
Throw him in!
The Mirror man gets his just rewards …

Franky, Ruby and Edi saved the day!
NOOOOOOOO
Now can we get something to eat?
But they never went into another Hall of Mirrors.

Sausage AND Carrots

Simone Lia

Explorer Stanley Sausage is the first to reach the summit of Saser Kangri - the tallest unclimbed mountain in the world.

He has climbed for weeks in freezing conditions, battling with mental and physical exhaustion.

Here he is, ready to put the flag in to show that he was the first sausage to reach the top.

Joke:
What is bright orange and sounds like a parrot?

A carrot!

Riddle:
Q. What has a mouth but cannot eat?

A. A river.